# THE REVOLUTION IN GENETICS

## UNDERSTANDING GLOBAL ISSUES

Published by Smart Apple Media
1980 Lookout Drive
North Mankato, Minnesota 56003
USA

This book is based on *The Revolution in Genetics: Where will biotechnology lead?*
Copyright ©2000 Understanding Global Issues Ltd., Cheltenham, England.

**Library of Congress Cataloging-in-Publication Data**

The revolution in genetics / edited by Patricia Miller-Schroeder.
  p. cm. -- (Understanding global issues)
Includes index.
Summary: Discusses advances in the study of genetics, such as the
discovery of DNA, the Human Genome Project, agricultural biotechnology,
and genetic engineering, and looks at the ethical implications these
technologies present.
  ISBN 1-58340-171-7
 1. Genetics--Juvenile literature. [1. Genetics.] I. Miller-Schroeder,
Patricia. II. Series.
  QH437.5 .R48 2002
  576.5--dc21
                                                    2001008450

Printed in Malaysia
2 4 6 8 9 7 5 3 1

**EDITOR** Diana Marshall          **COPY EDITOR** Heather Kissock
**DESIGNER** Terry Paulhus         **PHOTO RESEARCHER** Nicole Bezic King
**TEXT ADAPTATION** Patricia Miller-Schroeder

# Contents

# Introduction

Many exciting discoveries in the physical sciences have changed the world, beginning with Isaac Newton's discovery of gravity in 1687. Now in the 21$^{st}$ century, biological sciences are combining with technology to expand human knowledge. The field of science known as biotechnology is changing industry, health care, and the ways in which food is produced.

Developments in these areas have been possible since the discovery of a molecule

*DNA is fundamental to life on Earth and is found in every living creature.*

called deoxyribonucleic acid (DNA). DNA is found in every living creature, from microscopic single-celled bacteria to complex human beings. Fundamental to life on Earth, each DNA molecule is built like a chain, linking together the secret of life. Within the DNA are **genes**—tiny units of inheritance that make each living creature unique. Genes determine the physical characteristics of an individual, such as the markings on a cat's fur or the color of human hair.

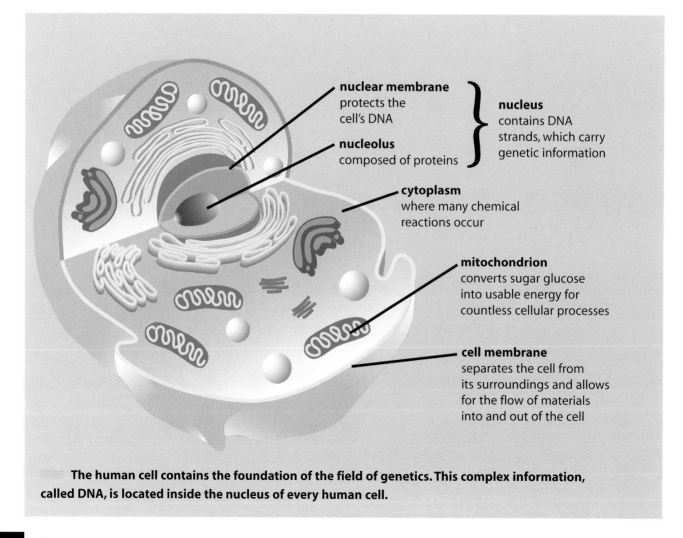

**nuclear membrane**
protects the cell's DNA

**nucleolus**
composed of proteins

} **nucleus**
contains DNA strands, which carry genetic information

**cytoplasm**
where many chemical reactions occur

**mitochondrion**
converts sugar glucose into usable energy for countless cellular processes

**cell membrane**
separates the cell from its surroundings and allows for the flow of materials into and out of the cell

**The human cell contains the foundation of the field of genetics. This complex information, called DNA, is located inside the nucleus of every human cell.**

During the 1960s, scientists figured out that DNA was a code. Since then, they have discovered how to read and even rewrite parts of the code. Some scientists have gone one step further, learning how to change the code and create new organisms that would likely never occur naturally. Until the end of the 20th century, only a small fraction of the complete genetic code for most of the world's species was known. Since the beginning of the 21st century, scientists have been able to read the entire genetic makeup, or genome, for some species. The first genomes to be read were those of single-celled microbes, such as disease-causing bacteria. Today, scientists are very close to sequencing the complete human genome.

The Human Genome Project (HGP) was officially launched in 1990. Scientists from around the world began working together to sequence the complete DNA code needed to fully understand the makeup of a human being. Sequencing involves the complex process of ordering, or mapping, the different parts of DNA. This is a massive undertaking. As more is discovered about the human genome, the new information is shared with researchers looking for new ways to fight disease.

Scientists will soon be able to locate, read, and copy genes from one individual or species to another. This has led to social and environmental concerns over how this new knowledge will be used and who will control it. Although biotechnology has been practiced for thousands of years, through such methods as selective breeding, the mid-1990s introduced many food crops to the United States that had been genetically altered. Modifying

## *Biotechnology has been practiced for thousands of years.*

crop genes improved yields, increased disease resistance, and enhanced nutritional qualities. However, some people worry about eating these crops. By being publicly vocal, groups concerned about personal health and the environment have prevented many of these genetically modified (GM) species from being used in Europe. Consumers worldwide are demanding involvement in the decisions made about biotechnology, especially when they affect their health and welfare.

Genetic knowledge is being applied to many areas of human health. Soon, genetic screening may be used to identify individual health-care problems. Gene therapy could cure serious inherited diseases, such as muscular dystrophy. On the other hand, some people fear that screening processes could be used to keep people with genetic problems from getting jobs and insurance coverage. Many others fear that genetic knowledge will enable parents to choose the genes they want their children to have.

Since advances in biotechnology are surrounded by controversy, **developed countries**, such as the United States, have implemented rules to guide research programs in genetics and biotechnology. All new developments in these areas are carefully examined. Drugs that are created through the manipulation of genes are subject to stricter and more numerous regulations than other drugs. Despite these restrictions, companies can still profit from huge amounts of money that research in biotechnology generates. As a result, this industry has called into question many issues of genetic ownership.

The global market has provided opportunities for large companies to introduce genetically altered crops into **developing countries**, using their natural resources for worldwide trade. As some farmers become dependent on the company's seeds and chemicals, they become unable to grow other crops.

The varied applications of genetic engineering have forced governments to debate scientific progress. As scientists gain the power to read and change genes, political leaders and consumers will have to make informed decisions to ensure that this power is used wisely.

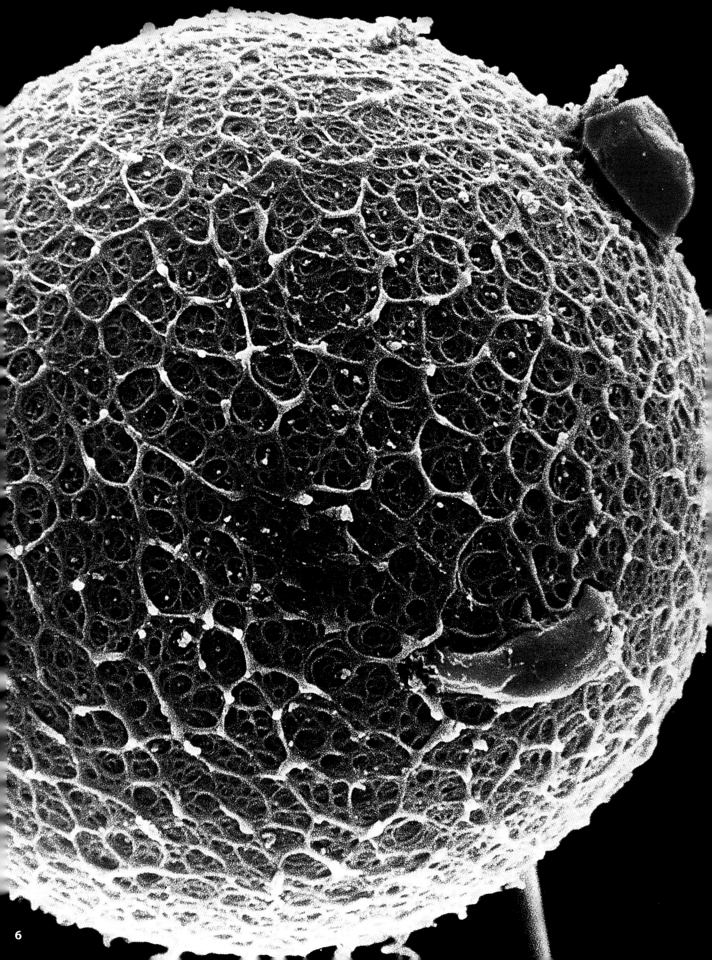

# The History of Heredity

Heredity, the process by which parents pass on characteristics or traits to their **offspring** through the transmission of genes, is older than human civilization itself. Thousands of years ago, the first farmers used their basic knowledge of this process to breed the plants that had the best features. Their goal was to produce higher yields and better quality food crops. Likewise, racehorse trainers and pigeon enthusiasts have long chosen the animals with the most desirable features for breeding. Ever since humans lived in communities, most people expected children to resemble their parents in some way.

Hippocrates, known as the Father of Medicine for his many early contributions as a physician, gave the first recorded explanation of heredity in 400 B.C. He suggested that each parent passed on important features of their bodies to their offspring. These features were contained in special particles that combined when a child was conceived. More than 2,000 years later, in the 1850s and 1860s, experiments performed by Gregor Mendel demonstrated

**The female egg (shown here) together with the male sperm transmit genetic information to offspring. This is where life begins.**

how traits were inherited. Mendel was a monk at a monastery in what is now the Czech Republic. At the time, the monks were studying and researching methods of improving crops and livestock. Mendel chose to study the garden pea. He crossbred peas that possessed different traits, such as green or yellow color, and smooth or wrinkled seeds.

*Hippocrates gave the first recorded explanation of heredity in 400 B.C.*

He noted the frequency with which the offspring in the next generation showed the various traits of each parent pea. From these simple experiments, Mendel created the first theory of how genes, which he called "factors," are inherited. Mendel's rules for genetic inheritance are still used today. While Mendel published his results in 1865, his work was not widely known until the early 20th century. It would be almost another century before the structure of DNA would be discovered, thereby solving the mystery of how genetic information is transmitted.

In 1859, Charles Darwin published *On the Origin of Species*. This book set out his

## CHARLES DARWIN

Born in Shrewsbury, England, on February 12, 1809, Charles Robert Darwin took after his grandfather, the well-known 18th-century physician, Erasmus Darwin. Young Darwin went to the University of Edinburgh to study medicine. In 1827, he dropped out of medical school and entered the University of Cambridge, where he learned how to observe natural phenomena. After graduation, at 22 years of age, Darwin worked as an unpaid naturalist on a scientific expedition around the world aboard the HMS *Beagle*.

Traveling to different regions of the world gave Darwin the opportunity to observe a large variety of fossils and living organisms. He noted, for example, that certain fossils of supposedly extinct species closely resembled living species in the same region. From his observations, Darwin explored the possible links between distinct but similar species of living organisms.

Upon returning to England, Darwin began his life's work on the changeability of species.

## THE LONG WAY

Giraffes evolved their long necks to reach food sources that were out of the reach of most animals. According to the process of natural selection, the giraffes that were born with naturally longer necks were able to reach higher up into the treetops for leaves. As a result, these longer-necked giraffes outlived the shorter-necked giraffes, who could not compete for food. From generation to generation, the long neck was passed on to descendants. Today, giraffes continue to use their long necks to find food in the treetops.

theory of natural selection, explaining that individuals with inherited traits that helped them adapt to their environment had a greater chance of surviving and reproducing. This process—popularly referred to as "survival of the fittest"—explained how species evolved. Some scientists, such as Darwin's cousin Francis Galton, thought that human behavior was inherited in the same way that Darwin's theory proposed physical characteristics were. They both believed that an individual's genetic inheritance was like destiny—unavoidable. Thus, certain people would be born to be geniuses, while others would be born to be criminals.

In thinking about the forms and habits that distinguish one species from another, most 21st-century biologists apply a perspective that consists of Darwin's ideas on evolution along with the genetic discoveries of Gregor Mendel. This new perspective is called neo-Darwinism.

## KEY CONCEPTS

**Deoxyribonucleic acid (DNA)**
A molecule of DNA consists of two chains. Strands composed of a large number of chemical compounds, called **bases**, are linked together and twisted into the shape of a winding staircase, called the double helix. DNA is the main constituent of the **chromosome**, and it carries the genes as segments along its two strands. DNA transmits genetic information from one generation of cells to the next. It also stores the sequence of bases that carry the information for the production of proteins necessary for cell function. Through these two functions, DNA connects today's human beings with their ancestors.

**Environmental influences**
Environmental influences are those which affect the body from the outside. Many animal rituals, such as mating, are influenced by their different environments. When the environment changes, so do the rituals. While human language and speech are organized by the brain, they are also taught externally by family

# NEO-DARWINISM

**The giraffe, the tallest living animal, can be found eating the leaves off trees in the East African woodlands.**

Today, humans are aware that both genes and environmental influences make individual human beings what they are, in a very complex combination.

Much of biology is interested in the ways in which species have developed their different forms and behavior patterns. Most modern biologists support the views of Darwin, a British naturalist of the 1800s. The ideas that resulted from Mendel's genetic inheritance theory are mixed with Darwin's classical theories about evolution and natural selection. This combination, called neo-Darwinism, broadens to include recent discoveries about DNA. Neo-Darwinism places much emphasis on DNA as the origin of all biological identity. Neo-Darwinists have modified Darwin's theory of evolution by stating that species evolve by natural selection as it acts according to genetic variation.

The father of neo-Darwinism, German biologist August Weismann, developed the germ-plasm theory of heredity in 1883. This theory separated the body's material from hereditary material, which he called the germ-plasm. His experiments confirmed this distinction by proving that acquired characteristics were not inherited.

The rediscovery of Mendel's work, around 1900, led to a modern synthesis of neo-Darwinism with genetics. Much of the evolutionary biology of the 20th and 21st centuries falls broadly into this category. Mendel's work proves that the determinants of evolutionary steps are not to be found in the physical world, but in the microscopic world of genes.

Some scientists broaden the scope of neo-Darwinism to include environmental influences on the evolution of species. In recent years, research has demonstrated that specific environmental signals can directly affect genetic structure, causing disease.

and region. Identity can be attributed in part to genetics, but behavior is often influenced by environment. Bacteria, which enter the body from the environment, can also alter gene expression, such as when pollution causes cancers.

**Evolution** The changes in a species or population that occur from generation to generation by mutation or natural selection form the process called evolution.

**Heredity** Heredity is the passing of biological traits, such as hair color, eye color, and body shape, from parents to their children through genes.

**Natural Selection** The process whereby the adaptation of a population to its environment is improved is called natural selection. Those best adapted to such things as climate change or competition for food survive and reproduce, passing on their genetic material.

# DNA Unraveled

While unraveling the DNA code was one of the 20th century's greatest achievements, present-day scientists are focusing on a different challenge—making sense of it. Necessary to this challenge is the thorough exploration of human genes and genetic functions.

It was already understood that the human body contains trillions of cells. Each cell, with the exception of red blood cells,

**Two coiled strands make up the double helix structure of all DNA molecules. This pattern contains the blueprint of life.**

carries a complete set of genes that make human beings what they are. This complete set of genes is the human genome.

*Unraveling the DNA code was one of the 20th century's greatest achievements.*

Genes are coiled along 23 pairs of tiny, thread-like chromosomes. In a newborn child, half of the chromosomes will be inherited from the female parent, while the other half will

come from the male parent. Each chromosome is made up of two chain-like strands of DNA. These strands are wound around each other into a spiral called a double helix. Each DNA strand is made up of four different bases. These bases are adenine (A), guanine (G), cytosine (C), and thymine (T)—the four letters that make up the genetic code. There are 3 billion of these letters in the human genome, forming about 31,000 genes. While very complex, the DNA from a single cell nucleus is much too small to be seen by the naked eye. However, if it could be uncoiled and tied together, it

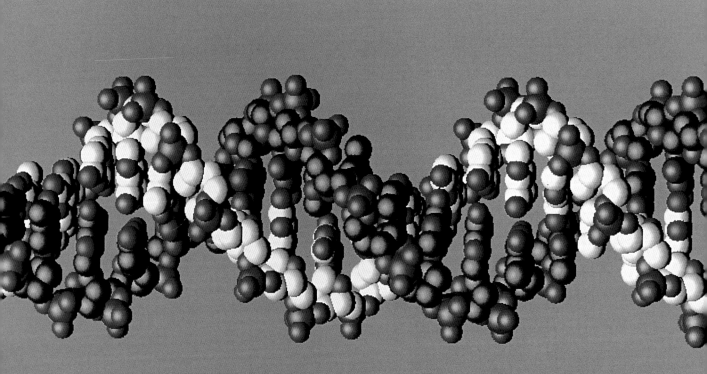

would measure almost six feet (1.8 m) in length.

The meaning of the sequences, which form genes, has taken much longer to figure out. Scientists have learned that each gene encodes a protein. The body needs tens of thousands of proteins. The human body uses them to build tissues, send messages to various organs, and aid in its chemical reactions. Proteins include insulin, which regulates the body's use of sugars, and collagen, which makes up bones and skin. Proteins are chains consisting of smaller units called amino acids.

The first step in making proteins is transcription, or the copying, of DNA into matching strands of another molecule, called **messenger ribonucleic acid (mRNA)**. The mRNA

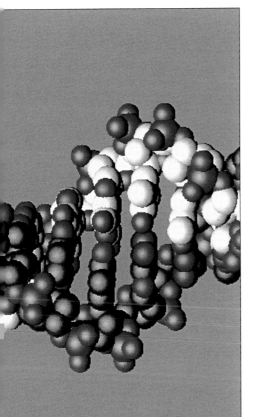

directs the cell's protein-manufacturing machinery, turning amino acids into proteins that the body needs. DNA instructs mRNA to produce proteins only when they are needed. From this process, scientists are beginning to understand the complex exchange of information between the cell and its environment. This information exchange determines which genes are translated into proteins, at any one time, to maintain a healthy body.

The process of protein production can be observed in the development of an **embryo**. All human beings begin life as a single cell. Yet, as adults, more than 100 different kinds of cells are found in the human body. While all of these cells perform different functions and produce different proteins, the functions are not pre-programmed. The cells pick up signals from their environment that tell them where to go in the embryo and what to do when they arrive.

Using Mendel's rules, classical geneticists established how traits, such as hair color, would be inherited. However, they could only describe the genetic makeup of an individual from the offspring's actual physical makeup. They were unable to determine how the cells picked up environmental signals until the genes were found. Finding the genes themselves was like finding an address in a large city without a map. Gradually, scientists began

## THE STRUCTURE OF LIFE

American biochemist James Watson and British biophysicist Francis Crick discovered the double helix structure of DNA in 1953. They realized that each base on a DNA strand always has the same partner on the opposite strand. Adenine always pairs with thymine, and cytosine always pairs with guanine. When the strands separate as cells divide, they can **replicate** their complementary strands. Replication is the key to life. It allows seeds to grow into trees and fertilized egg cells to develop into humans.

British chemist Rosalind Franklin found that DNA comes in two forms, which she called A and B. A colleague at King's College, Maurice Wilkins, showed an x-ray photograph that Franklin had taken of the B form to Watson. He saw that it supported a helical structure, and a few weeks later, he constructed the DNA model with Crick. Franklin preferred mathematical calculations that allowed her to interpret the x-ray photographs. Using this method, she arrived at the same result independently of Watson and Crick. Since Franklin died of cancer in 1958, Wilkins shared the Nobel prize with Watson and Crick in 1962, for their pioneering work on the structure of DNA.

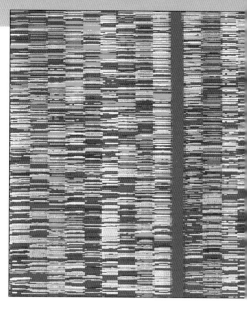

to find landmarks along the chromosomes. These landmarks are called genetic markers and are found throughout the DNA. Genetic markers are sequences that are very distinct. They provided the first entries on the genetic map of the human genome.

Since genes that caused inherited diseases were linked to some of the genetic markers, researchers soon realized that combining efforts would speed up the important process of finding disease genes. In 1990, the international genetics community launched the Human Genome Project. The project was dedicated to publishing a continuously updated map of the locations of markers and known genes of the human genome. The ultimate goal was not simply to locate the genes on the

*Researchers realized that combining efforts would speed up the process of finding disease genes.*

chromosomes, but to decipher their sequences as well.

One of the first scientists to efficiently sequence the DNA code was two-time Nobel prize-winner Fred Sanger from Cambridge, England. His findings were published in 1977. At the time, it was a huge step forward, but the process was slow by modern standards. Much faster methods were needed to

## HUMAN GENOME PROJECT

While the ideas behind the Human Genome Project (HGP) were being formulated in the mid-1980s, it was not until 1990 that it was officially launched in the United States. The HGP is an international research project that seeks to understand the entire genetic blueprint of a human being. The specific goals of the HGP are to construct a detailed genetic and physical map of the human genome, and determine the complete base sequence of human DNA. The human genome constitutes the basic set of inherited instructions for the development and functioning of a human being.

Through sequencing, the HGP has identified nearly all of the estimated 31,000 genes in the nucleus of a human cell and mapped the location of the genes on the 23 pairs of human chromosomes. Many scientists believe the HGP has the potential to revolutionize medicine by providing insights into the basic biochemical processes that underlie human diseases, especially inherited diseases.

The National Institutes of Health and the U.S. Department of Energy have been coordinating the project together. The project was originally planned to take about 15 years to complete, but effective resources and technological advances have accelerated the expected completion date to 2003 from 2005. In fact, in June 2000, a rough draft of the DNA sequence of the human genome was published—the entire human genetic code. The draft provided a basic outline of about 90 percent of the human genome. Researchers stated that 97 percent of the genome had been mapped, with 85 percent of the code accurately sequenced. All that remains is to fill in the gaps and correct the errors. The high-quality human genome sequence is expected to be complete by 2003. Scientists hope that by using the project's information, a new approach to medicine can be taken whereby faulty genes can be corrected.

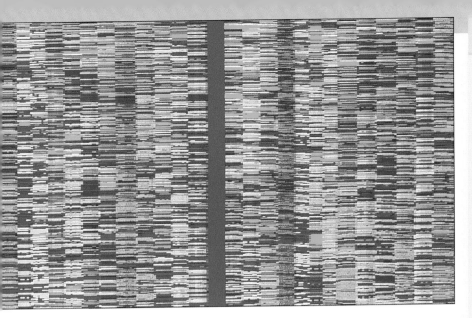

- Each human genome contains about 31,000 genes.

- There are 100 trillion cells in the human body.

- Each person has 23 pairs of chromosomes. By contrast, each mosquito has 3 pairs and each carp has 52 pairs.

- More than 95 percent of the human genome is "junk DNA."

- Human DNA is 99 percent identical to chimpanzee DNA.

- One strand of DNA measures about six feet (1.8 m) in length, but only 50 trillionths of an inch ($1.27 \times 10^{-12}$ m) wide.

- If the DNA in the human body was put end to end, it would reach to the sun and back more than 600 times.

- At any given time, the Human Genome Project (HGP) funds about 100 separate principal researchers.

- Since it began, the HGP has cost an estimated $3 billion.

- A rough draft of the completed human genome was announced in June 2000.

- Every second, HGP computers decode 12,000 letters in DNA sequences.

examine the billions of DNA sequences in humans and all the other animal and plant species that were of current interest. In 1986, automated genome-sequencing machines were invented. These machines use dye to tag the known segments of DNA, which results in a simple reading of the colors. The rate of sequencing in the late 1970s was several hundreds of bases per month. With the new machines, scientists can now sequence several million bases per week.

One of the first successful genome sequencings was that of the tiny **nematode worm**. This success convinced funding agencies in the United States, Europe, and Japan to invest in the Human Genome Project. Hundreds of millions of dollars would be needed to carry out the goal of this project. Finally, in December 1999, the sequencing of Chromosome 22—one of the smallest—was completed. In 2000, the rough draft of the entire human genetic code was revealed, causing

**The output from an automated DNA sequencing machine maps out the different segments of DNA in different colors.**

international debate and speculation. The complete sequence, without any gaps, is expected sometime in 2003.

The project has spawned a new field of research called bioinformatics. This science uses the power of computers and the Internet to analyze and distribute the sequence information. Bioinformatics developed in order to address the computing challenges raised by the Human Genome Project. Creating public databases connected to the Internet made genome data available worldwide, along with analytical software for making sense of this complex information.

Science is gaining new knowledge of human and other genomes daily. This knowledge is driving the genetics revolution of the 21st century.

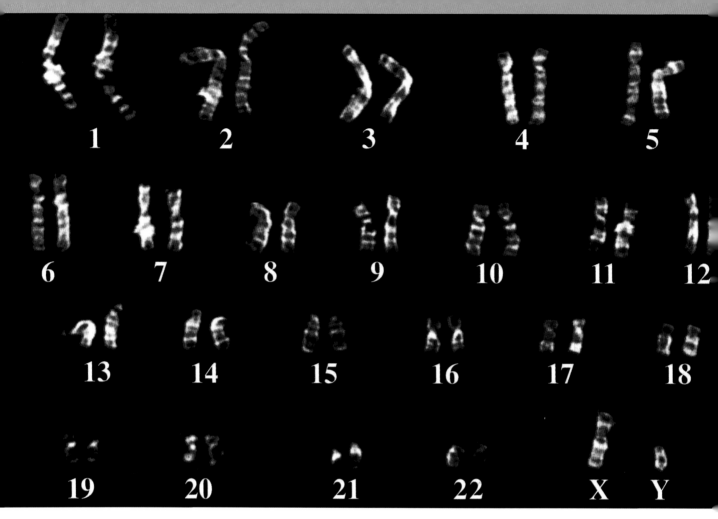

1  2  3  4  5

6  7  8  9  10  11  12

13  14  15  16  17  18

19  20  21  22  X  Y

A karyotype is a map of a cell's chromosomes. This male karyotype shows the number of chromosomes found in normal human cells—23 pairs.

## KEY CONCEPTS

**Amino acids** There are about 20 types of amino acids, called alpha amino acids, that serve as the building blocks of proteins. The function of a protein is determined by the sequence of its amino acids. A sequence of three bases is the genetic code word, or **codon**, that specifies a particular amino acid. For example, the codon for lysine— an amino acid essential for human nutrition—is AAG.

**Genetic markers** Distinctive DNA sequences are used as landmarks in mapping studies. While they consist of the same short sequence repeated over and over again, each marker comes in a number of slightly different variations. If everyone in a family that suffers from an inherited disease also has the same variety of a particular marker, then there is a good chance that the defective gene is near the marker. This linkage is the first step to finding disease genes. Markers can also provide the basis of the genetic fingerprinting technique used in criminal science, which matches the markers to DNA in blood or tissue samples.

**Genome** A genome is a complete sequence of bases making up the DNA of a single organism. It includes both sequences that constitute genes and direct the production of proteins, and other sequences that have no known function, sometimes misleadingly called "junk DNA." In humans, junk DNA represents about 95 percent of the total makeup of the genome.

# Biography
# James Watson

**Born:** April 6, 1928, in Chicago, U.S.
**Education:** Bachelor's degree of science, in zoology, at the University of Chicago, and Ph.D. in zoology at Indiana University
**Legacy:** Discovered the double helix structure of DNA and confirmed that DNA carries hereditary information by making copies of itself

Navigate to the Nobel e-Museum Web site: www.nobel.se/medicine/laureates/1962/ for information on related Nobel prizes. Also click on www.time.com/time/time100/scientist/profile/watsoncrick.html for more information about James Watson.

# People in Focus

James Dewey Watson went to local grammar and high schools in Chicago. He later entered the University of Chicago, where he received a bachelor's degree in zoology in 1947. As a young boy, his interest in bird-watching progressed into a serious desire to learn genetics. This became possible through graduate study at Indiana University, in Bloomington, where he received his Ph.D. in zoology in 1950.

During a 1951 conference in Naples, he met Maurice Wilkins. For the first time, he saw the x-ray photograph that directed his work towards the structural makeup of nucleic acids and proteins. Together with Francis Crick, he discovered the complementary double helical structure of DNA in March 1953.

The discovery of the structure of DNA is thought to be one of the most important biological discoveries ever made, opening up the field of genetics for the progress to come. In 1962, Watson and Crick, along with Maurice Wilkins, were awarded the Nobel Prize in Physiology or Medicine.

Watson went on to study the general principles of virus construction before becoming a member of the Harvard Biology Department. Working as a professor, his major research interest was the role of RNA in protein synthesis.

In 1968, Watson was the director at the Cold Spring Harbor Laboratory. His students discovered the molecular nature of cancer and identified cancer genes for the first time.

From 1988 to 1992, at the National Institutes of Health, Watson was the head of the Human Genome Project.

# Tools for Technology

Brewers, bakers, and cheese makers were the world's first biotechnologists. They used microbes to break down raw materials and turn them into palatable food items. The **enzymes** or chemicals produced by the microbes were used to produce bread, beer, and cheese. During the 20th century, chemists developed methods for large-scale **fermentation**. At the time, the beer and wine industries were major economic forces in France. By perfecting the scientific process involved in brewing and by culturing the right organisms, chemists were

*Cracking the genetic code opened the possibility of putting microbes to work for human benefit.*

able to decrease the likelihood that these beverages would sour. This increased overall production. These methods provided the right environments for microbes, such as yeasts and bacteria, to multiply and produce useful chemicals, such as alcohol. Massive-scale biotechnology industries thrived long before anyone had heard of genetic engineering, and their main tool was microbial activity.

Cracking the genetic code opened the possibility of putting microbes to work for human benefit. Scientists can now manipulate the DNA in microbes to produce certain proteins. For example, a human gene can be introduced into bacteria. The bacteria's protein-manufacturing machinery treat the human gene like one of their own, translating it into protein. The bacteria begin manufacturing the protein specified by the gene. In this

▨ **This scientist uses three-dimensional goggles and advanced computer technology to research possible applications of *E.coli* proteins in biotechnology.**

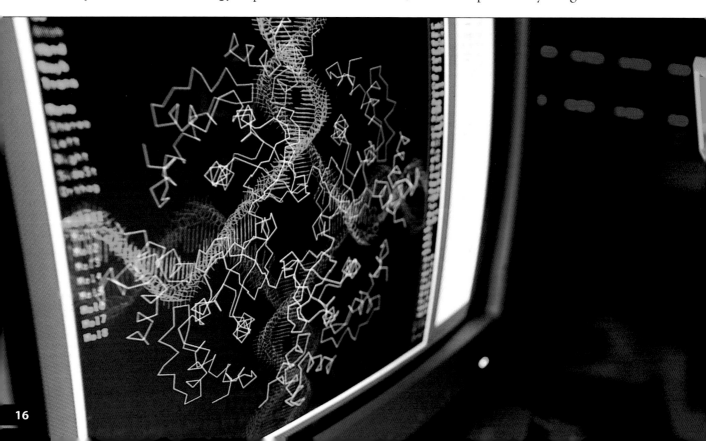

An ordinary-looking sheep named Dolly made the front pages of newspapers around the world in 1996. Her creation fueled fears about human cloning.

## HELLO DOLLY

In July 1996, a sheep called Dolly became the world's first mammal to be cloned from the cell of an adult animal. Scientists removed the nucleus from an egg cell taken from an ewe. It was replaced with the nucleus from an udder cell of another ewe. The resulting embryo was then implanted into a third ewe. This technique is called nuclear transfer and does not require fertilization. Dolly was the only survivor of more than 277 embryos created this way.

By the time Dolly reached three years of age, it was revealed that her cells were typical of a much older sheep—likely the same age as her mother. Researchers were unsure about whether this would cause her to die prematurely. On April 23, 1998, Dolly gave birth to a daughter named Bonnie. The birth of Bonnie proved that Dolly was not just a successful living clone, but that she succeeded in growing and maturing to the adult stage and was capable of producing healthy offspring. However, a report in January 2002 revealed that Dolly had developed arthritis, which is rare in five-year-old sheep. This news called into question the safety of animal cloning by linking the cloning process to genetic defects, and refueled the cloning debate.

way, microbes became the first targets of attempts to manipulate genes—the microbes themselves provide the tools for the job.

Taking DNA out of a living cell is no longer a difficult task. College students regularly attempt this task in biology laboratory work. However, finding a desired gene, removing it, and putting it into another organism is still a very complex maneuver. The first task is to cut the DNA into small fragments. During the 1960s, scientists discovered that bacteria produced enzymes designed to do just that. These enzymes are used to defend the bacteria against invading viruses. Called restriction enzymes, they cut the DNA at specific sites along the strand in such a way that leaves one strand longer than the other. This makes what scientists call a sticky end. One sticky end can be joined to another complementary sticky end on another DNA sequence.

There are many useful enzymes in the genetic

engineer's toolbox—most come from bacteria. Some cut DNA sequences and stick them back together. Others provide bases for sticky ends or repair damage so the new sequence can function. Bacteria also provide the means to insert a copy of a gene from one organism

▨ *E.coli* **bacteria, found in the human digestive tract, are being used in DNA research to produce the gene for human insulin.**

into another, solving the next major challenge of any genetic engineer.

A bacterium's cell has some of its DNA contained in a small loop called a plasmid. The plasmid operates independently of the chromosomes and is capable of genetic replication and gene transfer. Plasmids are exchanged between one cell and another in a bacterial colony. This makes the plasmid a perfect vehicle to carry a new gene

into bacteria. Scientists use enzymes to cut the plasmid open and insert the new gene before closing it up again.

Mixed with a culture of bacteria, these genetically engineered plasmids invade their new host bacteria. From there, they are passed on to future generations as the colony multiplies. While the colony grows in number, scientists need to select only bacterial cells that have the new gene. They usually

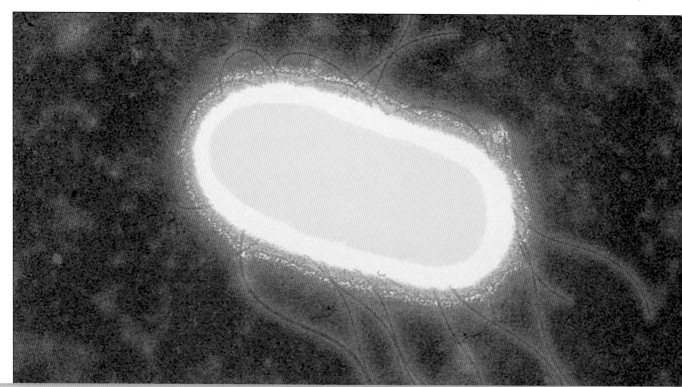

## KEY CONCEPTS

**Biotechnology** The science that uses living organisms or biological systems to create drugs or manage the environment is called biotechnology. By manipulating biological organisms, humans have been able to make beneficial products to aid food production, waste

disposal, mining, and medicine. Biotechnology has enabled the transfer of specific genes from one organism to another, the maintenance and growth of plant and animal clones, and the fusing of different types of cells to produce medical products.

**Clone** A clone is a copy of a living being that has the same genes as one parent. In sexual reproduction, offspring are created out of the mixing of both male and female genes. A clone has only one set of genes, making it identical to the one parent. Clones have specific desirable

do this by inserting an antibiotic-resistant gene into the invading plasmids. The whole colony is then treated with the antibiotic. Only the cells that carry the new genes will survive. These genetically engineered bacteria form a new colony, ready to be used in biotechnology.

Called recombinant DNA technology, this relatively new process was developed in the early 1970s. It has since been used to produce tons of new drugs and chemicals each year. One of the earliest and most widely used products of recombinant DNA technology was human insulin. Before this development, **diabetics** were treated with insulin taken from the pancreas of cows or pigs, which is similar but not identical to human insulin. The technology has also produced a blood-clotting protein to treat **hemophiliacs**. This protein had previously come from donated human blood, which carried with it the risk of viral infections, such as hepatitis C. Biotechnology has also produced growth hormones, which used to be extracted from

human corpses, to treat growth disorders. In some people, the human source caused a fatal brain condition.

Medical treatments are not the only products of transformed bacteria. The food industry uses many enzymes. The most widely known of these is called non-

animal rennet, which is used to make vegetarian cheese. Traditionally, cheese is made using the enzyme rennet, extracted from the stomachs of calves. Since food technologists have been able to insert the calf gene into bacteria, unlimited supplies of rennet can now be

## NEW BIOTECHNOLOGY DRUG AND VACCINE APPROVALS IN THE UNITED STATES BY YEAR

Advances in genetics have resulted in a significant increase in the drugs and **vaccines** created through biotechnology. In most years, the number of approved vaccines rises steadily.

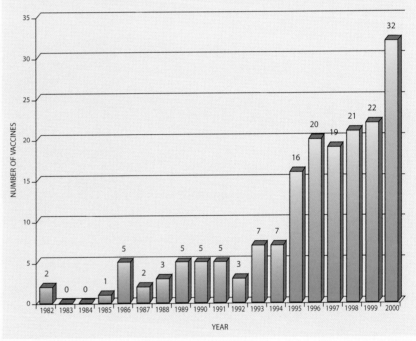

characteristics. Scientists can control what is produced by selecting the genes that go into a clone's DNA. For instance, a cow with high milk yield could be beneficial as a clone.

**Genetic engineering** Also called biogenetics, this science develops

and applies scientific procedures and technologies that allow manipulation of genetic material to alter hereditary traits. It is now possible to genetically engineer insulin by introducing the gene into bacteria and harvesting them to produce the hormone.

**Microbes** Microscopic bacteria, especially those that are disease-causing, and other microorganisms are called microbes. Microbes provide the tools for genetic engineering, allowing humans to manipulate genetic material.

Natural oil-eating bacteria can be used to clean up the more than 100 million gallons (455 million L) of oil that spill each year. Oil spills poison animals and clog birds' feathers, making it impossible for them to fly.

produced without killing any animals. Bacteria have also been engineered to clear up oil spills, absorb toxic metals, and generally clean up the environment.

While bacteria pioneered the recombinant DNA revolution, almost any living species can be manipulated into accepting foreign genes. Most animals and plants do not have plasmids. However, viruses are naturally designed to enter the DNA of the cells they infect. Viruses treated with biotechnology can be used as vehicles for transporting genes. Gene guns

*Almost any living species can be manipulated into accepting foreign genes.*

have also been developed that fire particles coated with DNA directly into cells. The quest to harness living things for human requirements seems to grow daily. Plants can make plastics and motor fuel. Sheep can be engineered to produce human proteins in their milk. It seems that biotechnology has no limits. What is permitted in the realm of biotechnology will depend on the limits imposed by laws and international regulations. The task now is for humankind to decide what is safe, necessary, and ethically justified.

# Biotechnologist

**Duties:** To find medical solutions by combining engineering and biology

**Education:** A bachelor's degree in relevant sciences, often along with a Ph.D.

**Interests:** Health care, developing new techniques and products, and a basic concern for human health and the environment

Navigate to the Biotechnology Industry Organization Web site: www.bio.org for information on related industries and careers. Also click on career.bio.com/pages/index.cfm for more information about biotechnology jobs.

# Careers in Focus

Biotechnologists use a combination of engineering and science to create new products, such as vaccines or foods, from biologically based raw materials. They can also develop factory processes that, for example, reduce pollution or treat water products.

Some biotechnologists spend much of their time studying, examining, and analyzing microorganisms, such as bacteria, fungi, and yeast. Others may operate and maintain equipment that is used for the processing of biological materials, such as pharmaceuticals and foods. Biotechnologists may specialize in one or several areas: the development and testing of new products, the genetic modification of organisms or foods, the monitoring of data, the study of the effects of waste materials on the environment, and many others. Biotechnologists can work in the medical field or strictly in research—in academic research centers, medical centers, or commercial industry companies. Biotechnology can be applied to manufacture pharmaceuticals, search for disease-causing genes, and even to help solve crimes by analyzing blood samples.

Biotechnologists are scientists that must be experts in their field and in using technology. Their jobs often require extensive computer knowledge and the ability to analyze digital data. The industry is widespread and growing very rapidly—a biotechnologist could work anywhere in the world, depending on his or her specialty.

Today, much of the biotechnology research is conducted in the drugs and pharmaceutical sectors, as these are highly profitable.

# Genetics and Medicine

**M**any of the treatments used in hospitals today were discovered accidently. Penicillin is a good example: In 1928, Alexander Fleming had been growing bacteria in unwashed dishes. He noticed that mold growing on the dishes stopped the bacteria from reproducing. Through this observation, it was discovered that the active agent, penicillin, was fantastically powerful at curing bacterial infections. However, scientists did not understand how the antibiotic worked until much later. The idea that, by studying

> *By studying the biology of a disease, scientists can develop a precisely tailored cure.*

the fundamental biology of a disease or the agent that causes it, scientists can develop a new, precisely tailored cure is quite new. Since scientists can now read the human genome and the genomes of disease-causing organisms, a new realm of possibilities for curing and even preventing disease has been opened up.

Researchers can find and sequence genes that cause certain inherited diseases, making it possible to develop genetic tests for those likely to be susceptible to the disease. It might also be possible to develop gene therapy, where individuals with the disease could receive a healthy gene to replace the faulty or absent one. Yet another possibility would be

**Penicillium mold produces the common antibiotic penicillin.**

# THE CRUELTY OF GENETIC DISEASES

Two of the most common inherited diseases are cystic fibrosis and muscular dystrophy. Both of these affect young people and can lead to early death. Each disease results from a fault in a single gene. This could be a misspelling in the genetic code or a genetic sequence missing altogether. Either way, the gene fails to make a vital protein. The genes for both of these diseases were discovered and sequenced in the late 1980s.

Cystic fibrosis causes the lungs to become clogged with mucus, leading to infections and breathing difficulties. It affects 1 in 2,500 children, but 1 in 25 people has the defective gene. To develop the disease, a child must inherit the affected gene from both parents. If only one copy of the gene is inherited, illness does not result. However, the gene will be carried.

Muscular dystrophy is a crippling disease of the muscles. It usually affects males since it is carried on the X chromosome. Males receive an X chromosome from their mothers and a Y chromosome from their fathers. Females receive an X chromosome from each parent. If a girl inherits the muscular dystrophy gene from her mother, the normal gene from her father allows her to remain healthy. However, she still carries the defective gene. Each of her male children will have a 50 percent chance of being born with the disease.

to design a drug that compensates for the faulty gene.

There are many beneficial applications for genetic testing. A genetic test tells whether an individual has a gene defect that causes disease. However, until there are cures for these diseases, a positive result in a genetic test can raise difficult personal or ethical questions. A person may be well, but his or her relatives may have a genetic disease. That person could take a test to find out if he or she is a carrier. For, while many people carry many of the disease-causing genes, only a fraction of them will display symptoms. People who know they carry the cystic fibrosis, muscular dystrophy, or Parkinson's disease genes may want their partners to take a test before starting a family with them, to avoid passing the gene on to their offspring.

Since the early 1990s, another option has been available to some parents who are carriers of disease genes—preimplantation diagnosis. This involves creating several embryos through **in vitro fertilization**. A cell from each embryo would be tested, and only those embryos without the gene defect would be placed in the mother's womb. The first baby born using this technique was delivered in London, England in 1992. She was born healthy to parents who both carried the gene for cystic fibrosis.

Gene therapists develop treatments based on the replacement of faulty genes with healthy ones. The difficult part of this process is inserting the healthy genes into the exact spot where they are needed. Many clinical trials have been in progress since 1990 in the United States, and elsewhere in the world. These trials have involved thousands of patients. Gene therapy experiments have been conducted for various genetic conditions, including cystic fibrosis, some types of cancer, and genetic disorders of the **immune system**. Doctors have established that it is possible to carry new genes into the body in viruses or oil droplets. New genes are delivered to cells in the blood or the lining of the nose and lungs. So far, the results of these trials have not been spectacular and there are no long-term cures in sight.

Some researchers would like to try germ line gene therapy. Involving the insertion of healthy genes into an embryo at an early stage of development, this would affect not just the cells in that embryo, but the cells of all of the embryo's descendants as well. This technique has been attempted

# PREDICTING DISEASE

Many experts believe that the genetic discoveries of the 20th and 21st centuries will lead to the ability of doctors to predict disease in individuals. With the ability to read full genetic profiles—as a result of the Human Genome Project—diseases will become detectable before they even start.

By the end of the 20th century, there were more than 450 tests for human genetic disorders, and the number has been steadily increasing. Genetic testing will tell a person whether he or she is susceptible to particular disorders or diseases. This knowledge would allow individuals to make informed lifestyle choices, such as quitting smoking cigarettes or eating certain foods, and alter their behavior accordingly.

Already, researchers have discovered the genetic causes behind Alzheimer's disease and some cancers, among many others.

While often life-threatening, diseases caused by a defect in a single gene are quite rare. In recent years, genetic research has focused more on common disorders, such as cancers, heart disease, asthma, and diabetes. Growing evidence confirms that genes influence a human being's chances of having these conditions. In these cases, it is likely that several genes interact in complex ways to cause the disease. Once complete, the knowledge gained from the Human Genome Project will enable researchers to look for genetic differences between individuals who have these conditions and those who do not. Soon, doctors will be able to show patients their genetic profiles and provide information on their probability of suffering from a variety of diseases. With this information, some patients could be given drugs to prevent or slow the progress of a disease. Others might be advised to change their lifestyles by altering their diet or increasing their exercise levels.

in laboratory and farm animals. However, the results have not always been successful. In September 2000, the American Association for the Advancement of Science (AAAS) released a report calling for a period of delay on all attempts to cure genetic diseases by altering the genome that would be passed on to an offspring. Concluding that human germ line gene therapy would be unsafe and unethical, the AAAS believed that neither science nor society was ready for the implications of this type of research. Proposals have been made outlining the necessity for a national group or agency to study safety and ethical issues associated with the field. No such group exists, so germ line therapy on humans remains forbidden in the U.S. Still, some researchers argue that it is the only way to eliminate disease.

# KEY CONCEPTS

**Gene therapy** The treatment of disease through the replacement of damaged genes with functional ones is revolutionizing medicine. By 2020, as many as 5,000 diseases will be screenable through genetic processes. From curing some types of diabetes to the replacement of body parts, gene therapy attempts to cure disease before it begins to damage the body. Laboratories are being set up worldwide to research cures for chronic diseases and immune system illnesses that are often caused by a single defective gene.

**Germ line gene therapy** Out of the breakthroughs in genetic research, molecular biology, and technology emerges the possibility of modifying human genes to be transmitted to future generations. While this would gradually and systematically eradicate some diseases, the procedure is controversial.

**Pharmaceuticals** Hundreds of new medicines, from painkillers to cancer treatments, are produced by pharmaceutical companies

Studying the genetics of organisms that make people sick has given a new push toward finding vaccines for infectious diseases. Increasingly, microbes are becoming resistant to drugs. This is the case with the bacteria that cause tuberculosis and the parasites that cause malaria. These two microbes kill millions of people worldwide each year. New diseases, such as HIV/AIDS, are also becoming major killers. Vaccines are being developed that use copies of the disease-causing microbe's own genes to attack and fight off the microbe. The genes are inserted into a modified virus or bacterium to create a vaccine, or are injected directly as DNA. Once injected into the body, the body's own cells take up the disease DNA and make proteins from it. This causes an immune response in the body that protects it from future infection.

A controversial genetic engineering procedure can create animals that have enough human genes to fool the human immune system, so the animals'

each year. However, it takes years for a new product to become commercially available. Drug trials are conducted using volunteers, and if the results are successful, the government must approve the product. The entire process, from research and laboratory work all the way to the drugstore shelf, usually takes about 12 years.

## CURES FOR CANCER

A cancer is a group of cells that grows out of control. While there are some cancers that are harmless, or benign, many others are malignant and can have fatal results. Early detection and drug therapy are currently the best ways to treat a cancerous tumor.

Possible cures are being developed for cancer from the increase in knowledge of the functions of two genes—DNA-PK, which normally repairs damaged genes, and P53, which stops damaged genes from reproducing themselves. When either gene is lacking or has mutated, the possibility of developing cancer increases.

Among the hopes for a cure is the genetically engineered P53 gene. Much like a missile finds its target, this gene is designed to seek out and find cancerous cells. Another genetic possibility involves injections that starve cancerous cells in the body by interrupting the glucose that stimulates their growth.

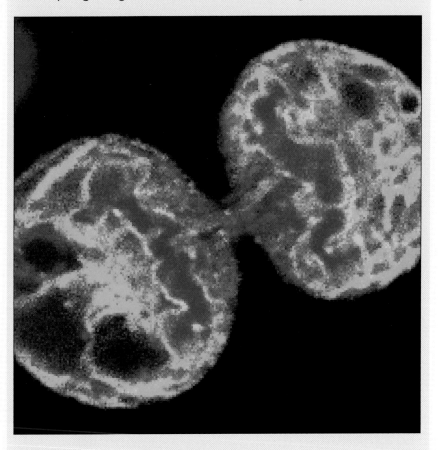

Replacing mutated cell growth control genes with normal cell growth control genes could prevent these skin cancer cells (shown above) from reproducing.

In December 2001, a ruling from the Human Fertilisation and Embryology Authority (HFEA) in England made it possible for a British couple to select in vitro fertilization babies according to whether they could provide a cure for their other child, who suffers from a fatal blood disorder, called thalassemia.

The HFEA reported that it was acceptable in some cases to check embryos to see if they are a tissue match for an existing child. They argued that the ability to select embryos to become potential donors could save many children who currently suffer from incurable blood disorders. During in vitro fertilization, a number of embryos are created using eggs and sperm taken from a mother and a father. By taking tiny samples from the developing embryos, couples will be able to select those that would be compatible as a donor.

While the HFEA approved this particular case, it stated that future uses of this procedure would have to be assessed individually. The British Medical Association (BMA) approved the ruling, but cautioned against using the procedure at the physical risk of child donors.

organs can be transplanted into humans without the risk of rejection. Developers of this technology claim that transplanting animal organs is necessary—there are simply not enough human organ donors. Some companies have already bred pigs with certain human genes for this purpose. Still, many people have concerns about the safety of this procedure. Others are concerned about the welfare of the animals used.

Medical research into gene use began in university laboratories. Now, there are hundreds of small biotech companies. Millions of dollars depend on the development of gene sequences and technologies.

▨ **Since their organs are the right size for humans and they breed quickly, pigs are favored animal donors.**

Giant companies that control most of the world's pharmaceutical industry are also investing in biotechnology. Some experts predict that biotechnology will eventually cure disease and slow down aging. Others claim that humans will be able to control their own evolution. Still others forecast that genetic technology will be used to boost intelligence, athletic ability, and even physical attractiveness. Whether or not these claims are realistic remains to be seen.

# Clinical Geneticist

**Duties:** To trace and identify genetic mutations, disorders, and diseases

**Education:** A degree in genetics or a related science and a medical degree (M.D.)

**Interests:** Concern for patient health care and an interest in the molecular makeup of organisms

Navigate to the HGP Careers in Genetics and Biosciences Web site: www.ornl.gov/hgmis/education/careers.html for information on related careers. Also click on www.faseb.org/genetics for more information about genetics jobs.

# Careers in Focus

Clinical geneticists have a medical degree and are specialized doctors. While attending medical school, most students major in the biological or physical sciences. After medical school, a residency in pediatrics, obstetrics-gynecology, or internal medicine is usually completed, followed by a fellowship in clinical genetics. Individuals are then qualified as clinical geneticists. They work in research centers, hospitals, or medical centers. Many clinical geneticists work at university medical centers. A smaller number have private practices. Some dermatologists, pathologists, and dentists are clinical geneticists. Some clinical geneticists practice gene therapy.

Great strides are being taken in several areas of human genetics. Geneticists are gaining a deeper understanding of the basic functions of genes. They are able to determine how the basic functions in some genes go awry. On the job, a clinical geneticist's main responsibility is to recognize and identify genetic disorders and birth defects. They evaluate the implications of their diagnosis for the patient and provide access to proper treatment. They may also help the patient understand and cope with the disorder—offering various forms of counseling. Clinical geneticists generally specialize in certain areas. Some clinical geneticists work mainly with infants and children. Other clinical geneticists focus on genetic problems in fetuses.

New advances in technology are giving way to new methods of diagnosis and treatment. An important role of the clinical geneticist is to act as the link between the scientists who are making technological advances in diagnosis and treatment, and the patients who may benefit from these advances.

# Mapping the Genetically Modified World

## Figure 1: Worldwide GM Crops

By 2000, the number of countries cultivating GM crops on a commercial scale had grown to 13. Of these, the United States remains by far the largest grower—about 68 percent of American soybean crops were genetically modified in 2001. Many more countries, including the United Kingdom, have undertaken small-scale trials of GM crops as part of the process of evaluating their environmental safety. However, public debate on labeling issues seems to be strengthening the need for regulation and research before new products are commercially introduced.

 canola

 corn

 cotton

 potato

 soybean

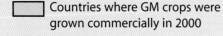 Countries where GM crops were grown commercially in 2000

GERMANY

FRANCE

ROMANIA

SPAIN

CHINA

SOUTH AFRICA

AUSTRALIA

# Charting Genetics

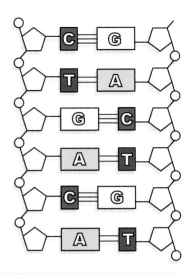

### Figure 2: The Double Helix

The double-stranded DNA molecule is held together by chemical components called bases. Adenine (A) always bonds with thymine (T) and cytosine (C) always bonds with guanine (G). These letters spell out the code of life. About three billion base pairs make up the entire human genome. They code approximately 31,000 genes.

### Figure 3: The Human Genome

Twenty-three pairs of chromosomes, which vary in size, hold the complete set of genes that makes up a human being. Genes are located in particular positions on the chromosomes, and the goal of genome mapping is to pinpoint these locations. Genome sequencing goes one step further, reading the complete sequence of bases that make up the genes and the junk DNA between them.

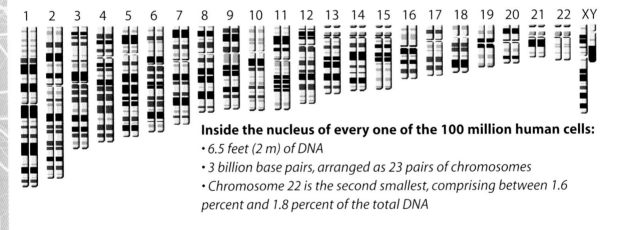

**Inside the nucleus of every one of the 100 million human cells:**
- *6.5 feet (2 m) of DNA*
- *3 billion base pairs, arranged as 23 pairs of chromosomes*
- *Chromosome 22 is the second smallest, comprising between 1.6 percent and 1.8 percent of the total DNA*

### Figure 4: Mendel's Law

Mendel's experiments with garden peas revealed the principles of heredity (shown right). The crossing between the red and the white flowers gives a generation of hybrid pink flowers, which are intermediate in color between the two parents. These pink offspring, when crossbred, give red, pink, and white flowers in an average proportion of 1:2:1.

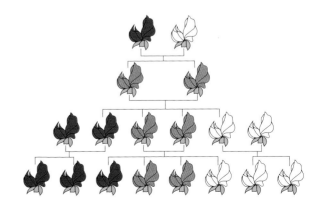

## Figure 5: An International Collaboration

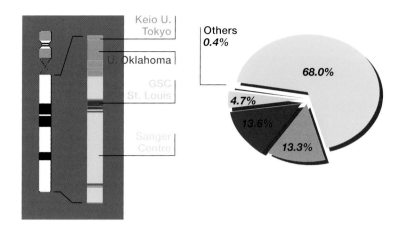

The major part of the work was done by the Sanger Centre, a non-profit research institute in Cambridge, England, funded by the Wellcome Trust. Important work has also been done by research centers in the U.S. and Japan:

Keio University, Tokyo, Japan
University of Oklahoma, U.S.
Genome Sequencing Center, St. Louis, U.S.

**With the collaboration of the Chromosome 22 mapping community:**

The Children's Hospital of Philadelphia, U.S.
University of Alberta, Edmonton, Canada
Albert Einstein College of Medicine, New York, U.S.
Cal Tech, Pasadena, U.S.
Karolinska Hospital, Stockholm, Sweden

The Human Genome Project is an international effort. The largest contributors to its funding are the Departments of Energy and the National Institutes of Health in the U.S., and the Wellcome Trust in the U.K. France, Germany, and Japan have also made contributions. This non-profit research occurs in sequencing centers worldwide. Results are made available to other researchers via the Web.

## Figure 6: Global Land Area Planted in Biotechnology Crop Varieties by Country (2000)

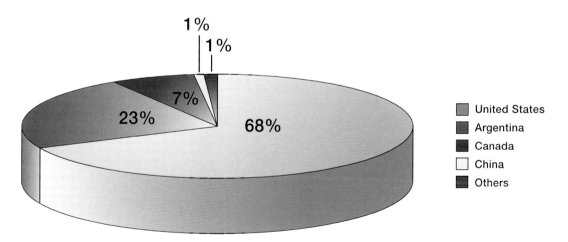

**Total global area: 109.2 million acres (44.2 million hectares)**

The United States continues to be the largest grower of biotechnology crops. Increasingly, this area is expanding. In 1996, the U.S. reported 3.7 million acres (1.5 million h) of biotechnology crops. By 2000, biotech crops increased to about 74.9 million acres (30 million h). Major crop varieties found in the U.S. are soybeans, corn, and cotton. Argentina's primary biotechnology crop is soybeans, while Canada's is canola. Biotech cotton is China's primary modified crop.

# Down on the Farm

Farmers have been manipulating the genes of food crops and domestic animals for thousands of years. Called selective breeding, this technique involves breeding only those varieties that have the most desirable traits. Modern wheat, oats, barley, and corn are quite unlike their ancestors. The dairy cows and pigs of today differ from the wild oxen and boar of earlier times. In the 20th century, plant breeding became a science rather than an art.

Through the use of **pesticides** and **fertilizers**, today's crops have incredibly high yields. However, it is unlikely that modern agriculture can sustain such high food production for long. The chemicals used in agriculture— called agrochemicals—depend on non-renewable resources, such as oil, and damage the environment if used for prolonged periods. Farmers worldwide spend more than $8 billion each year on chemical **insecticides** alone. Yet, up to 40 percent of crops are still lost to pests and diseases. Recent developments in agricultural

biotechnology have made it possible to produce plants with their own defenses against insects. Plants can be tailored to suit other purposes as well: to tolerate salt or drought, resist herbicides, or delay ripening.

> *Plants can be tailored to tolerate drought, resist herbicides, or delay ripening.*

Biotechnology is faster than conventional methods, such as selective breeding, which occurs over generations. It can also target one specific desired gene and insert it into the plant in one shot. While most of the genes used to modify crops come from bacteria or plants, this may soon change. Researchers can now introduce genes from unrelated species. These genes are taken from a particular species that would never naturally breed with the other because of their dissimilarity. For example, an experiment demonstrated that genes from cold-water fish can protect fruit from frost damage.

Companies have engineered crops to include the natural insecticide *Bacillus thuringiensis* (Bt) in the plants themselves. They have also produced crops that are resistant to the weed-

killing herbicides that they manufacture. The companies argue that this enables farmers to wait until weeds appear before spraying. As a result, less weedkiller is needed, and when it is needed, crops are unharmed. A more controversial technology is called the "terminator gene," which was patented in the United States in 1998. Inserting this gene into engineered crops stops them from producing fertile seeds. This prevents accidental escape of the genes into other plant species. However, farmers would not be able to save seed from one year's crop to plant the next. While many farmers in developed countries buy new seed every year anyway, seed saving is a traditional part of farming in many countries. Seed saving is considered a right by conventional plant breeders.

Reducing the use of chemical sprays through genetically modified (GM) crops would have clear environmental benefits. However, the usual aim of biotechnology is to increase profits for farmers and the companies that supply them. The technology could be used to bring advantages to consumers, such as the strains of rice that have been developed to produce high levels of vitamin A and iron. Children who live in countries where rice is the staple

**By 2002, GM canola began appearing in farmers' fields where it was not even planted. Since the engineered crop can resist conventional herbicides, it has proven impossible to control.**

food often have low levels of vitamin A and iron. Recent research has been done on bananas to genetically engineer them to produce vaccines. Since vaccines need to be kept in a cool place, this would be especially useful in tropical countries where cold storage is limited.

Progress in the production of GM food crops has been very rapid. In 1992, tobacco farmers in China were planting crops with altered genes that increased disease resistance. By 1994, the Flavr Savr slow-ripening tomato was approved for sale in the United States. The following year, 12 more GM products were available to consumers. By the end of 1998, 40 GM crops were approved for sale in the U.S. In 2001, 68 percent of American soybeans were genetically modified, up from 54 percent in 2000. GM varieties accounted for about 26 percent of the corn and 69 percent of the cotton planted in 2001.

In Europe, the story has been different. Swiss, French, and German consumers have rejected

▨  **Due to public concern, transgenic tomatoes are no longer available in supermarkets in the United States.**

GM foods almost from the beginning. Tomato paste made from genetically engineered tomatoes went on sale in British supermarkets in 1995. It was clearly labeled and was cheaper than the non-GM tomato paste. The product outsold the non-GM alternative. This changed when the media began reporting on GM foods, stating that the American soybean that was used in up to 60 percent of processed foods was very likely genetically modified. Suppliers claimed that it was impossible to keep GM and non-GM soy

apart. Consumer groups raised concerns about the possible environmental and health risks of GM foods. They demanded that all food containing GM ingredients be labeled. The campaigns have been very successful in Europe and are now being held in the U.S. Regulations on labeling are being considered in the U.S. Few European countries have approved commercial growing of GM crops. As a result, American farmers are finding few international markets for their produce.

## KEY CONCEPTS

**Biodiversity**  Many experts warn that genetic modification of crops and livestock threatens essential biodiversity. This variety of plants and animals in an environment is important in maintaining its proper functions.

**Bacillus thuringiensis (Bt)**  Bt is a bacterium that lives in soil and

produces a range of natural and specific insecticides. It is available commercially to organic farmers—who avoid synthetic chemical pesticides—to spray on their crops. Biotechnology companies in the United States have taken its use a step further by incorporating Bt genes into such crops as corn, cotton, and

potatoes, thus removing the need to spray at all. Environmentalists fear that pollen from Bt crops could poison wildlife, such as butterflies.

**Food standards and regulations**  The Food and Agriculture Organization (FAO) of the United Nations believes in both the

# GENETICALLY MODIFIED FOODS

| ADVANTAGES | DISADVANTAGES |
| --- | --- |
| Food quality can be improved and controlled. | Genetically modified foods are not natural. |
| Food processing would be less expensive and much easier. | Genes could escape from crops into related wild species. This could create indestructible weeds. |
| Crops can be protected from weeds, diseases, and insects, thereby reducing the need for chemical pesticides. | Wildlife could suffer by losing the biodiversity that provides their food and shelter. |
| With increased productivity of crops, more of the world's increasing population can be fed and nourished. | Antibiotic-resistance genes, sometimes used in biotechnology, may find their way into bacteria. The microbes could become immune to the antibiotics used in treating disease. |
| Modified strains of crops could prevent diseases or treat nutritional deficiencies in the developing world's human population. | Introduced genes in foods might cause unforeseen allergies and other side effects. |
| The minimal disturbance caused by the farming of genetically modified crops could reduce topsoil erosion. | Large companies owning both GM technology and agricultural chemicals could threaten to control the world's food supply. In addition, consumer choice in food would be limited. |
| Crops can be genetically modified to thrive in unfavorable environments. As a result, world populations could better use their resources. | Wildlife could be directly poisoned from the altered crops. The monarch butterfly is already suffering from the Bt toxin in corn crops. |

The genetic revolution seems to have progressed too far and too fast for many consumers. They want answers to questions about safety and environmental protection. Scientific research and international food regulations are attempting to answer these questions. GM crops may have to be produced more cautiously in the future, offering clear benefits to consumers and not just to producers.

beneficial and destructive potential of GM foods. Having recently established various international commissions, it supports a science-based evaluation system to determine the benefits and risks of each individual GM organism. The FAO has called for a case-by-case approach to the exploration of concerns relating to the biosafety of each product prior to its release. It also encourages national regulatory authorities to clear each new GM product.

**Transgenic** A species of plant or animal that has received a gene or genes from another species, so that it will exhibit a desired characteristic, is called transgenic. While capable of producing a wide range of benefits in crops and livestock, many fear this process will threaten the environment by disturbing the existing balance between organisms and the biodiversity upon which they depend.

# Genetics and Ethics

Society has been influenced by genetics in many ways. Darwin's cousin, Francis Galton, one of the fathers of the science of genetics, was also a founder of the eugenics movement. Eugenics sought to "purify" the human genetic legacy. It tried to prevent those they thought to be genetically inferior from reproducing. In the early 20th century, eugenics policies were introduced into parts of the United States, Canada, and Europe. Hundreds of thousands of people were

*A hole has been made in this human embryo to allow the removal of a cell for genetic testing.*

*History tells of many instances of misuse of genetic principles.*

classified as being unfit. Often these people belonged to ethnic or racial minorities, while others were merely poor. Those in power hoped to create what they considered to be an orderly society. In many places, people thought to be genetically unfit faced compulsory sterilization—individuals were no longer able to produce children and thereby pass on their genes. During the Nazi reign in Germany, Nazi policy took the principles of genetic purification one step further than sterilization—extermination. This resulted in the deaths of millions of Jewish people, shocking the rest of the world into reconsidering eugenics policies. History tells of many such instances of misuse of genetic principles.

Today, humankind has the power to change the future genetic landscape in much more

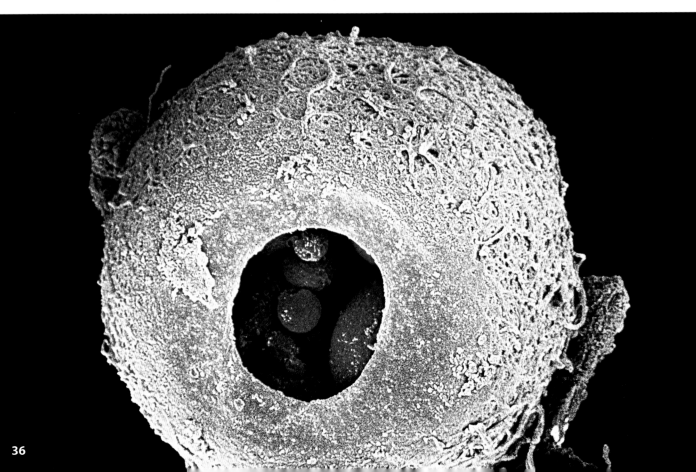

beneficial ways. In considering past abuses of human rights, societies must question how this power should be used. Many people are unsure as to whether it should be used at all. A large number of people worldwide are opposed to genetic technologies. There are widely held feelings that it is morally wrong to alter living beings, and that to upset nature's order is dangerous. However, moral arguments can also favor genetic technology, arguing that it has the potential to cure disease or provide food for the hungry. In the past, there was widespread moral objection to blood transfusions and organ transplants. As time passed, and new evidence of their benefits emerged, this changed. Now, most people accept such procedures on the basis that they save lives.

Even if it is agreed that there is nothing wrong with the transfer of genes, there are still decisions to be made based on how human science should use genetic technology and genetic information in the future. A balance between the goals of society and the rights of individuals must be maintained. Decisions must be made with the knowledge that they will affect the lives of people and other species far into the future.

Genetic screening could provide individuals with detailed information about their genetic health. Armed with this type of information, individuals would have the chance to make lifestyle

# THE GENETIC DILEMMA

### Fingerprinting and DNA analysis
Genetic fingerprinting is an accurate means of identifying individuals. It has been used to obtain convictions in criminal cases. Some police forces want to keep all such records, regardless of whether individuals are innocent or guilty. This would help with future crime detection. Others argue that to hold such information on citizens who have not committed any crime is a violation of their civil liberties.

### Discrimination
The possibility of improving our genes poses many ethical dilemmas, including the possibility that genetic testing may be used to discriminate. Some people already discriminate against others because of their race, class, or gender. Many believe that genetic makeup might soon be added to that list. Discrimination could also be applied to unborn children who are known to carry genetic diseases.

### Germ line cells
It is now possible to modify the DNA of germ line cells—those cells that are passed on from generation to generation. Many argue that this is tampering with the natural processes of evolution. Germ line cell modification will bring with it a new set of ethical dilemmas.

changes, take preventative medications, or get treatment. However, the fear is that others could use the information to discriminate against people believed to carry genetic risk. This has already happened. In

> *A balance between the goals of society and the rights of individuals must be maintained.*

the early 1970s, a screening program for **sickle cell anemia** was developed. African Americans who were found to be carriers of the defective gene

were penalized. Even though they were healthy, they still had a hard time getting jobs and health insurance.

Technology is already being used to screen embryos for genetic defects. This allows parents the choice of aborting their unborn baby if it is suffering from a serious genetic disease. It is now also possible to diagnose and discard test-tube embryos that have faulty genes, implanting only those genes that are healthy into the mother during in vitro fertilization treatments. Some argue that it is morally wrong to allow a seriously disabled child to be born when it is possible to prevent it. Parents and children across the United States and Great Britain have already brought cases to the courts for "wrongful life." The claim is that if the parents had been correctly advised of the child's likely condition, they would have terminated the pregnancy. However, such a view devalues the lives of disabled individuals. Many people with disabilities live happy and fulfilled lives.

While it is possible today to permanently alter the genetic makeup of a child, soon it may be legalized. Such genetic changes would be passed on to the child's descendants, using technology to correct genetic disease. The temptation for parents to use this technology to enhance their child's intelligence, athletic ability, or physical attractiveness might arise. Many wonder whether the genes for these qualities should even be identified.

While many research scientists are motivated by the desire to find cures for diseases or improve the quality of human life, the development of genetic technologies often lies in the hands of big businesses. Their main concern is often profit. Individuals with unusual genetic conditions often volunteer to participate in research programs. In the past, they have been upset by what happens to this research—large corporations sometimes obtain the rights to commercial development of genes discovered in the research. Similar outcries have followed

## FIRST HUMAN CLONE

On November 25, 2001, Advanced Cell Technology, Inc. (ACT), based in Worcester, Massachusetts, announced that it had completed a human embryo clone.

ACT used nuclear transfer methods pioneered in animals to create the embryo clone. The human eggs were encouraged to start dividing on their own, without fertilization or the transfer of genetic material. The process, known as **parthenogenesis**, occurs in insects and microbes.

The cloning technology will be used to grow a tiny ball of cells, which can then be used to produce stem cells. ACT stressed that its aim is to use the technology as a source of stem cells. The stem cells would be used to create life-saving therapies and treat diseases, ranging from leukemia and AIDS to such degenerative disorders as heart disease.

American politicians responded to the announcement and ensuing debate with a plan to outlaw human cloning. President George W. Bush repeatedly stated that human cloning should be made illegal. While United States Federal law already prohibits the use of tax dollars to fund the cloning of humans, ACT is a privately funded organization. The announcement of the first human clone provoked debate worldwide.

claims made by major companies from the developed world on the biological resources of developing countries.

*Many scientists are motivated by the desire to cure disease or improve the quality of human life.*

Indigenous communities have cultivated plants, such as the neem tree and basmati rice, over thousands of years, only to have major commercial companies now lay claim to these resources.

Genetic manipulation of non-human animals raises many animal welfare issues. Many transgenic animals, usually mice, are created in laboratories to study basic biological and disease processes, and to test new treatments. Their genes may be engineered to reproduce symptoms of fatal diseases, such as cancer. Animal-rights supporters argue that such experiments cause the animals to suffer. For this reason, they argue that experiments are not justified, even if they result in cures for human diseases. Some farm animals are genetically modified to increase milk yields or to increase the amount of

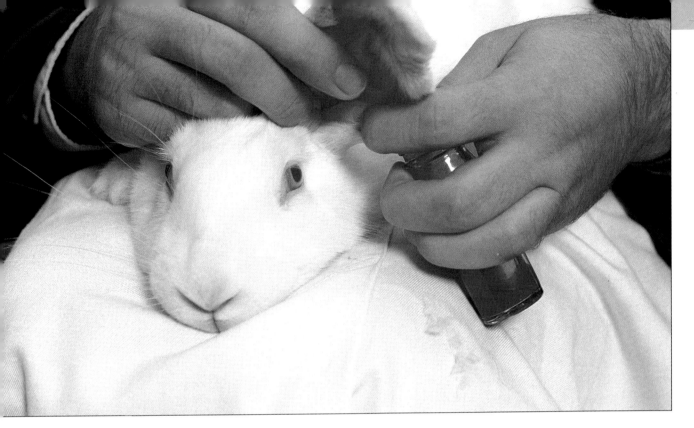

lean meat on a carcass. Genetic improvement of farm animals also raises concerns about the welfare of the animals. A pig genetically engineered in the United States to grow faster and produce leaner meat developed severe health problems. It could not bear its own weight and was crippled by arthritis.

The budget for the Human Genome Project includes funding from several countries for research into the ethical, social, and legal aspects of the project. It is now widely agreed that the scientific and business communities should not have sole responsibility for exploring the ethical questions. The wider community must be involved in the debate through education and public consultations.

**Laboratory researchers collect regular blood samples from the central artery of rabbits' ears. The blood samples are then analyzed to reveal changes or abnormalities.**

## KEY CONCEPTS

**Eugenics** Out of the 21ˢᵗ century's genetic developments emerges one of the most controversial issues—genetic eugenics. Scientific discussion has focused on the possibility of handpicking the genes of unborn children. Science is now able to manipulate disease-causing genes, altering the future of unborn children. Soon, parents may have the opportunity to produce designer babies, selecting certain traits, such as physical strength or intelligence, that they desire. Many geneticists are concerned that genetic techniques will remove the element of chance and randomness that exists in nature. Scientists are predicting that in less than 50 years, it will be easy to add 100 genes into an embryo at one time. The fear is that diversity will decrease, and that a race of superhumans will emerge, widening the gaps in the range of genetic makeup.

**Human rights** Human rights are considered fundamental to modern society. They are the basic rights of an individual and include the right to be born, the right to live, the right to work, and many others. Some geneticists, such as Mary-Claire King, have devoted large parts of their careers to human rights issues.

# THE STEM CELL DEBATE

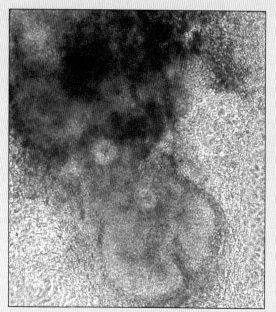

These embryonic stem cells have been programmed to form a beating heart muscle.

Stem cell research has caused much debate worldwide. Stem cells are young cells, found in embryos, that have the ability to develop into any of the body's 130 different types of tissue. Researchers in this field hope that by growing such cells in laboratories, they will be able to program them to produce specific tissue, such as kidney, heart, or even brain tissue. This tissue would then be used to repair damaged organs in living humans. In November 2001, a major breakthrough in stem cell research rekindled the debate: two separate research groups succeeded in making stem cells from human embryos develop into brain cells, opening up the possibility of treatments for diseases such as Alzheimer's and Parkinson's. The debate often concentrates on the source of these stem cells: they either come from fresh human embryos obtained from fertility treatments or abortions, or embryos cloned specifically for their stem cells.

| PROS | CONS |
| --- | --- |
| Many scientists have argued that the use of tissue from stem cells would replace the often risky procedures of organ transplants. | Many groups are opposed to the destruction of human embryos, no matter how early it occurs in their development. |
| Therapeutic cloning, which involves the creation of human embryos through cloning, would create cells that are more likely to be accepted by the receiving patient's immune system. | Many people do not support the cloning of an embryo only to dispose of it once stem cells are removed. Furthermore, they worry that this procedure may lead to the creation of live human beings. |
| Researchers believe that stem cell research will result in treatments for distressing, incurable, and fatal diseases, including diabetes, leukemia, AIDS, and many other currently untreatable disorders. | President George W. Bush has publicly expressed fears that abuses in cloning power may result if human cloning is allowed. The House of Representatives has passed a bill outlawing human cloning. |
| Scientists are willing to work within strict regulations for stem cell research and cloning technologies. Some groups suggest that stem cell therapy should be permitted under rigid legal controls, which would enforce the ethical issues. | Skeptics are convinced regulations would be very hard to enforce. Some government officials from the United States have warned about the dangers of corporations opening embryo farms. |

# Biography
# Mary-Claire King

**Born:** 1946, in Chicago, Illinois
**Education:** Mathematics degree from Carleton College and Ph.D. in genetics at the University of California
**Legacy:** Proved that human and chimpanzee genomes are 99 percent identical and that breast cancer is partly hereditary

Navigate to the Federation of American Societies for Experimental Biology at www.faseb.org/genetics/gsa/careers/bro-03.htm for information on related human rights work. Also click on www.washington.edu/alumni/columns/sept96/king2.html for more information on King.

# People in Focus

Geneticist Mary-Claire King studies and identifies the genes responsible for common medical conditions. By analyzing human DNA, King has contributed to the study of breast cancer, lupus, and inherited deafness. Her research focuses primarily on finding hereditary links. Throughout her career, King's work has addressed political issues, such as human rights.

Her doctoral thesis revolutionized evolutionary biology. Through her study of proteins, she proved that human and chimpanzee genomes are 99 percent identical. This placed the divergence of the two species from a common ancestor at about 5 million years ago, rather than the 10 million years of previous thought. After receiving her Ph.D., King taught in Chile. She returned to the United States in 1973 to work in the Medical School of the University of California, where she became interested in the genetics of breast cancer. King was the first geneticist to prove that breast cancer is partly inherited, finding the genetic markers for a number of inherited breast and ovarian cancers.

King researched the sequencing of DNA to identify kidnapped children during Argentina's military dictatorship. As many as 200 children were kidnapped and given to families in the military. King helped some of the missing children find their families by tracing a direct genetic link to their maternal grandmothers using genetic markers. She proved kinship and reunited about 50 children with their families. For her humanitarian work, she received worldwide recognition.

# Who is in Control?

Scientists themselves were the first to express doubts and urge caution in the field of genetic engineering. In February 1975, a historic conference was held in California. Scientists from many countries agreed to suspend recombinant

**Genetic advances have solved many infertility issues. This six-day-old human embryo will be stored in a culture until it is ready to be implanted in the mother's womb.**

DNA research until the safety issues and ethical implications had been fully assessed. It was also decided that regulatory bodies needed to be established. Within a couple of years, the National Institutes of Health had set up the Recombinant Advisory Committee in the United States, while the British government set up the Genetic Manipulation Advisory Group. Other similar bodies around the world have developed guidelines for genetic research. Research resumed and continues to this

day within these regulations and guidelines.

A major concern expressed by many advisory groups is containment—the idea that altered genes must be physically prevented from escaping into the environment. Once researchers began to develop transgenic organisms that were specifically designed to enter the environment to kill pests, new rules and regulations were needed. Those organisms designed to be released into the environment, such as food

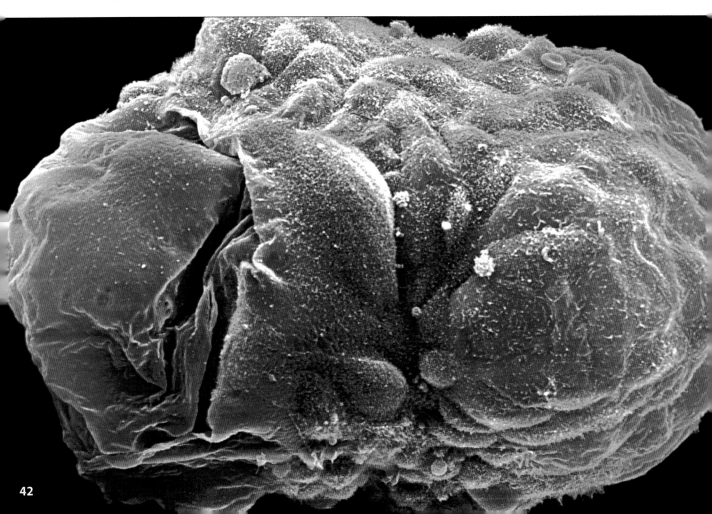

plants or viruses, required risk assessment. Such agencies as the Environmental Protection Agency, in the United States, and the Advisory Committee on Releases to the Environment, in the United Kingdom, work to ensure that environmental laws are being enforced. Any company that wants to test a genetically modified crop has to demonstrate that planting the crop will not harm the environment. If permission is granted, the company must report any adverse effects of the planting. These laws are in place to safeguard the health of consumers. In the United States, genetically modified food has to obtain the approval of the Food and Drug Administration (FDA) before reaching store shelves.

Critics argue that the rules and regulations are too weak. Authorities normally rely on safety tests carried out by the producing company; they do not carry out independent tests. They examine each case in isolation. Moreover, until recently, little thought was given to the long-term impact of GM crops on farming and wildlife.

Consumer choice has only recently become a consideration. The FDA made a decision in 1992 that angered consumers. They determined that food containing GM ingredients did not need to be labeled if those ingredients were "substantially equivalent" to the non-GM versions. While the narrow scientific definition of "substantial equivalence"

# PATENTING LIFE

Companies invest a great deal of money in isolating DNA sequences. They argue that they must be able to patent the sequences to recover their investment. This does not mean that they own all organisms containing that sequence, as some would argue. However, it does give them the exclusive right to its commercial development. The international patenting community has yet to resolve the issues surrounding companies wishing to patent parts of genetic sequences. While this would afford them total control in the creation of new products based on the sequences they isolated, international regulations would have to be in place to control future developments.

Patent laws vary from one country to another. The European Patent Office takes a much more cautious line than the United States over the issue of when a gene sequence becomes an invention. The first recombinant DNA patent on a microorganism, designed to clean up oil spills, was granted by the United States Patent and Trademark Office in 1980, after almost a decade of legal debate. Companies have since been granted broad patents, allowing them exclusive rights to all genetically engineered forms of a particular species, such as cotton. At least one company has successfully applied for a patent on a partial gene sequence whose function is unknown. Several hundred more applications are awaiting decisions. The applications are being hotly contested, and as a result, patent laws in this area are continuously evolving.

The publicly funded researchers working on the Human Genome Project have always opposed the patenting of human sequences. They argue that patent protection should be reserved for products that are made using the gene sequence, rather than for the sequence itself.

focused on the nutritional value of the food, it neglected the many other reasons why a consumer might choose not to buy GM products. In Europe, there was a mass consumer revolt against GM products in the late 1990s. As a result, labeling is now required for any food in which more than one percent of any ingredient comes from a genetically modified

source. By the end of 1999, the United States was again looking at the question of labeling. One year later, President Bill Clinton's administration tightened some of the regulations, but remained convinced that labels were unnecessary. By the end of 2001, American policy makers began to publicly express their disappointment with European Union-wide insistence that all

The 30,000 protesters at the 1999 WTO summit in Seattle brought international attention to a number of issues, including the development and control of biotechnology.

foods containing one percent GM ingredients be labeled. The battle continues today.

In the field of medicine, drugs produced through biotechnology must follow all of the regulations for genetically altered products. In addition, they have to follow the standard regulations for drug development. Their developers have to prove that the drug is effective and safe. Only then will it be licensed.

In the United Kingdom, extra controls have been introduced for gene therapy, which fall under the close scrutiny of the Gene Therapy Advisory Committee (GTAC). There are other advisory groups on human genetics, on genetic testing, and on in vitro fertilization. Each of these advisory groups includes members of the public on their committees. They also consult

## LEGAL MATTERS

On December 12, 2001, the United Nations (UN) General Assembly decided to establish a panel that will study and oversee the creation of an international convention against the reproductive cloning of human beings. Acting upon the recommendations of its legal committee, the UN General Assembly agreed that reproductive cloning threatened human dignity and should therefore be regulated by the international community's legal system.

the public on these very sensitive issues. A consultation carried out between 1998 and 1999 confirmed that the ban on reproductive cloning should stay in place and recommended that some limited cloning be reconsidered in five years, only if the technology used human tissue to advance medical research and treatment without producing fetuses or babies. By 2001, the governments of the United Kingdom and the United States both seemed to favor the banning of reproductive cloning.

On the wider international stage, regulation is overseen by a number of bodies with different interests, such as the World Health Organization (WHO), the Food and Agriculture Organization (FAO), and the World Trade Organization (WTO). However, the different nations of the world often cannot agree on the more controversial issues. In 1999, the WTO meeting in Seattle was divided on several issues. One was whether or not the WTO should be given the right to regulate international trade in GM crops. National governments, mainly from Europe, blocked this move, while the United States supported it. Since there is still a lack of international

## THE BIOSAFETY PROTOCOL

On January 29, 2000, 130 nations—including the United States, Canada, Australia, and the United Kingdom—agreed on the Biosafety Protocol. This will, for the first time, control international trade in genetically modified foods, animal feed, and seeds. The Biosafety Protocol was first proposed at the Convention on Biological Diversity in 1992, at the Rio Summit, where it was signed by 160 countries. Led by the United States, it took five years to negotiate and finalize. The Biosafety Protocol is a victory for environmental campaigners. It allows governments to ban imports of GM materials without having to provide scientific evidence that those materials cause harm. It will be enough to show that there is scientific uncertainty about the effects on health or the environment. The agreement also requires countries to cooperate on research into the environmental and health impacts of GM crops and foods.

agreement on issues such as food safety, labeling, environmental protection, and traditional

*Advisory groups control human genetics, genetic testing, and in vitro fertilization.*

resource rights, for now, the regulation of genetically engineered organisms remains at the national level.

This disharmony reflects the great difficulty in assessing the risks and benefits of genetic manipulation. Biotechnology is very new, very powerful, and developed with great speed. Governments and international agencies must decide how best to regulate it. They need to talk with scientists, business representatives, special interest groups, and consumers. A hands-off approach might unleash untold dangers. On the other hand, to be too cautious might deny medical and other benefits to millions of people worldwide. It is crucial that all parties involved in the debate be well informed.

## KEY CONCEPTS

**Patents** A patent grants inventors or developers the exclusive right to sell a product for a certain number of years. In genetic sequencing, much ethical debate centers around the distinction between patenting a product that results from gene sequencing and patenting the sequence itself.

# Time Line of Events

**circa 8000 B.C.**
Humans first domesticate crops and livestock.

**circa 2000 B.C.**
The Sumerians first use biotechnology to brew beer, leaven bread, and produce cheese.

**500 B.C.**
First antibiotics—moldy soybean curds—are used in China to treat boils.

**400 B.C.**
Hippocrates gives the first recorded explanation for heredity.

**A.D. 1322**
Arab chieftains first use artificial insemination to produce superior horses.

**1665**
Cells are first described by Robert Hooke.

**1675**
Antony van Leeuwenhoek discovers bacteria.

**1859**
Darwin publishes *On the Origin of Species*, in which he proposes his theory of evolution.

**circa 1866**
Gregor Mendel publishes the results of his experiments on garden peas, establishing the field of genetics.

**1879**
Alexander Fleming discovers chromatin, rod-like structures inside the nucleus of a cell, known today as chromosomes.

**1900**
*Drosophilas* (fruit flies) are used in early studies of genes.

**1944**
Oswald Avery demonstrates that DNA is the "transforming factor" and the material of genes.

**1946**
It is discovered that genetic material from different viruses can be combined to form a new type of virus—genetic recombination.

**1951**
Artificial insemination of livestock using frozen semen is successful.

**1953**
Watson and Crick discover the double helix structure of DNA. The modern age of biotechnology begins.

**1962**
Watson and Crick share the 1962 Nobel prize with Maurice Wilkins.

**1970**
Restriction enzymes that cut and splice genetic material are discovered.

**1973**
Stanley Cohen and Herbert Boyer perfect genetic engineering techniques to cut and paste DNA (using restriction enzymes) and reproduce the new DNA in bacteria.

**1977**
Fred Sanger finds the first efficient method of sequencing DNA code. Hundreds of bases can now be sequenced per month.

Chromosomes prepare to transfer the cell's genetic material into a new cell during the third stage of cell division called metaphase.

**1980**

The first United States patent for gene cloning is awarded.

**1980**

The first gene-synthesizing machines are developed.

**1981**

Scientists at Ohio University produce the first transgenic animals by transferring genes from other animals into mice.

**1983**

The first genetic markers for specific inherited diseases are found.

**1985**

Genetic fingerprinting enters the courtroom.

**1988**

Congress funds the Human Genome Project, a massive effort to sequence the human genome. The project does not officially launch until 1990.

**1990**

The first federally approved gene therapy treatment is performed successfully on a four-year-old girl suffering from an immune disorder.

**1992**

Scientists unveil a technique for testing embryos in vitro for genetic abnormalities.

**1994**

The first genetically engineered whole food approved by the FDA—the Flavr Savr slow-ripening tomato—is put on the market.

**1996**

The first clone to be born is a sheep named Dolly.

**2000**

The first agreement to control international trade in GM food, animal feed, and seeds is signed by 130 nations.

**2000**

A rough draft of the complete human genome map is produced, showing the locations of more than 31,000 genes.

**2001**

The first human embryo is cloned in the United States.

# Concept Web

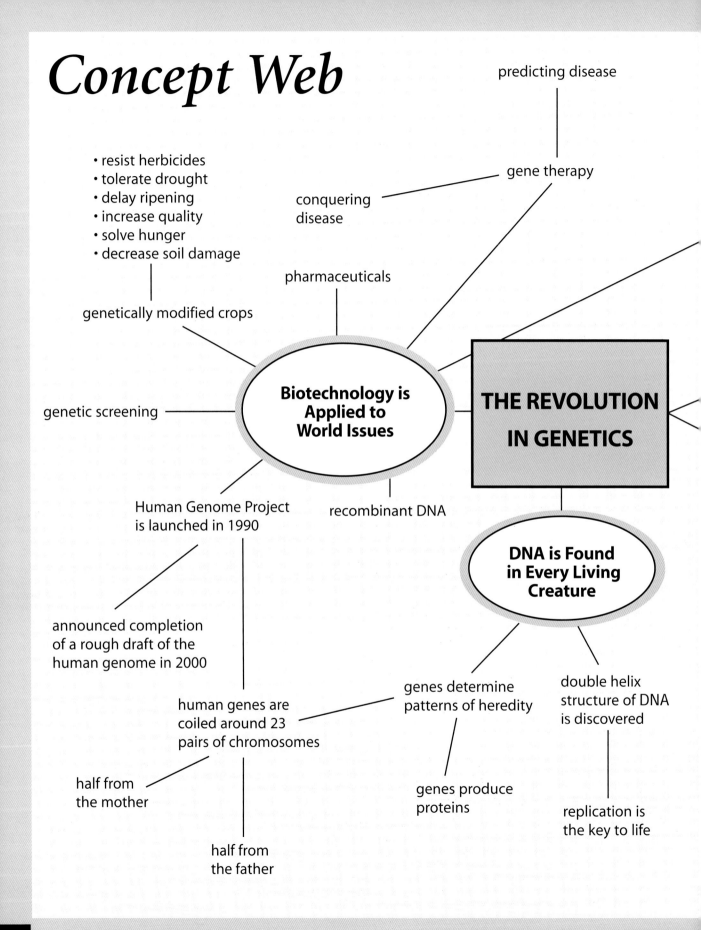

predicting disease

resist herbicides
- tolerate drought
- delay ripening
- increase quality
- solve hunger
- decrease soil damage

gene therapy

conquering disease

genetically modified crops

pharmaceuticals

genetic screening

**Biotechnology is Applied to World Issues**

**THE REVOLUTION IN GENETICS**

Human Genome Project is launched in 1990

recombinant DNA

**DNA is Found in Every Living Creature**

announced completion of a rough draft of the human genome in 2000

human genes are coiled around 23 pairs of chromosomes

genes determine patterns of heredity

double helix structure of DNA is discovered

half from the mother

genes produce proteins

replication is the key to life

half from the father

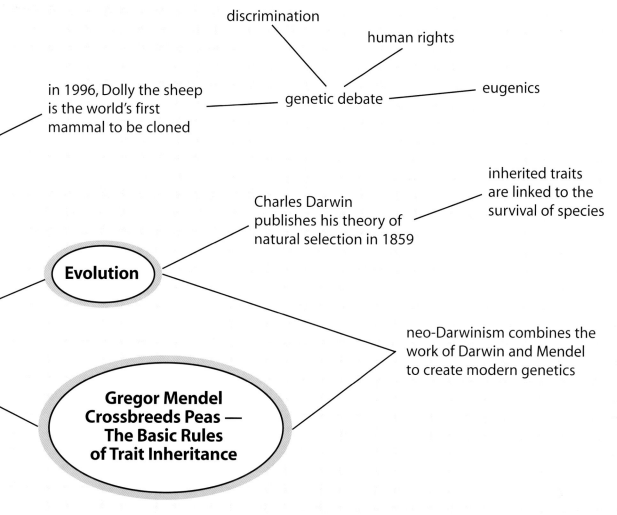

discrimination

human rights

in 1996, Dolly the sheep is the world's first mammal to be cloned

genetic debate

eugenics

Charles Darwin publishes his theory of natural selection in 1859

inherited traits are linked to the survival of species

**Evolution**

neo-Darwinism combines the work of Darwin and Mendel to create modern genetics

**Gregor Mendel Crossbreeds Peas — The Basic Rules of Trait Inheritance**

## MAKE YOUR OWN CONCEPT WEB

A concept web is a useful summary tool. It can also be used to plan your research or help you write an essay or report. To make your own concept web, follow the steps below:

- You will need a large piece of unlined paper and a pencil.
- First, read through your source material, such as *The Revolution in Genetics* in the Understanding Global Issues series.
- Write the main idea, or concept, in large letters in the center of the page.
- On a sheet of lined paper, jot down all words, phrases, or lists that you know are connected with the concept. Try to do this from memory.
- Look at your list. Can you group your words and phrases in certain topics or themes? Connect the different topics with lines to the center, or to other "branches."
- Critique your concept web. Ask questions about the material on your concept web: Does it all make sense? Are all the links shown? Could there be other ways of looking at it? Is anything missing?
- What more do you need to find out? Develop questions for those areas you are still unsure about or where information is missing. Use these questions as a basis for further research.

# Quiz

**Multiple Choice**

1. Chromosome 22
   a) was sequenced in December 1999.
   b) is one of the smallest chromosomes in the human genome.
   c) was a major step toward the completion of the Human Genome Project.
   d) all of the above

2. Dolly
   a) is a goat.
   b) was the first human to be cloned using cells from an adult animal.
   c) only has one parent.
   d) all of the above

3. Genetic markers
   a) are distinctive DNA sequences.
   b) are used as landmarks in mapping studies.
   c) are the first step to finding genetic diseases.
   d) all of the above

4. The Biosafety Protocol
   a) was signed by six countries.
   b) was proposed by the United States.
   c) controls international trade in genetically modified foods, animal feed, and seeds.
   d) all of the above

**Milestones**

Match the scientists with their genetic milestones.
   1. Gregor Mendel
   2. Mary-Claire King
   3. Watson and Crick
   4. Charles Darwin
   5. Hippocrates

   a) proposed the theory of natural selection.
   b) examined trait inheritance in garden peas to create the first theory of genetic inheritance.
   c) discovered that the human and chimpanzee genomes are 99 percent similar.
   d) first set out a theory of heredity.
   e) founded modern genetics by discovering the double helix structure of DNA.

### True or False

1. Patenting a genetic sequence gives companies ownership rights to all organisms containing that sequence.

2. In 1999, the WTO meeting in Seattle discussed whether the WTO should be given the right to regulate international GM crops trade.

3. In the United States, any food product that contains more than one percent of any ingredient from GM sources must carry a label.

4. By copying genes into bacteria, food technologists have been able to create vegetarian cheese.

5. If DNA could be uncoiled it would measure two feet (0.6 m) in length.

6. The nematode worm provided genetics with the first complete genome sequence of a multicelled organism.

7. "Survival of the fittest" means those species that are most physically fit will survive through reproduction.

8. Ninety-five percent of the human genome is "junk DNA."

Answers on page 53

Back Forward Stop Refresh Home Favorites History Search Larger Smaller Print Mail

Address: [▼] [                                        ] [↱ Go] [🔍 ▸]

# *Internet Resources*

**The following are Web sites dedicated to the pursuit of genetic progress:**

## HGP
http://www.ornl.gov/hgmis

The Human Genome Project Web site is the official source of information on the project and its progress. From introductory information about the HGP and its goals, to research, education, medicine, and ethical links, this site offers a complete guide to the project, along with all the breakthroughs and events of the past decade.

## Scientific American
http://www.sciam.com

Scientific American offers online reviews, news, and articles on all the latest scientific discoveries. Topics include the advances in biotechnology, cloning progress, reader's reactions, ethical considerations, and current events. The site offers many interesting features, including a section that directly answers any science question you may have.

## BIO
http://www.bio.org

The Biotechnology Industry Organization Web site offers news and features on recent developments in the highly complex field of biotechnology. Industry trends and up-to-date statistics on a wide range of topics are available at the click of the mouse.

**Some Web sites stay current longer than others. To find other genetics Web sites, enter terms such as "DNA," "biotechnology," or "clone" into a search engine.**

# Further Reading

Dowsell, Paul. *Genetics: The Impact on Our Lives (21ˢᵗ Century Debates)*. Austin: Raintree Steck-Vaughn, 2001.

Dudley, William. (Ed.) *The Ethics of Human Cloning (At Issue)*. San Diego: Greenhaven Press, 2000.

Hyde, Margaret O. and John T., Md. Setaro. *Medicine's Brave New World: Bioengineering and the New Genetics*. Breckenridge: Twenty First Century Books, 2001.

Marshall, Elizabeth L. *High-Tech Harvest: A Look at Genetically Engineered Foods (Impact Books: Science)*. New York: Franklin Watts, Inc., 1999.

Skelton, Renee. *Charles Darwin and the Theory of Natural Selection (Barrons Solutions Series)*. New York: Barrons Juveniles, 1987.

Watson, James D. *The Double Helix: A Personal Account of the Discovery of the Structure of DNA*. New York: New American Library, 1991.

## Answers

**Multiple Choice:**
1. d)   2. c)   3. d)   4. c)

**Milestones**
1. b)   2. c)   3. e)   4. a)   5. d)

**True or False**
1. F   2. T   3. F   4. T   5. F   6. T   7. F   8. T

# Glossary

**bases**: four nitrogen-containing compounds that form the building blocks of DNA or RNA

**chromosome**: microscopic thread that consists of DNA and protein, and contains genes

**codon**: three attached bases in mRNA that code for a specific amino acid in the production of protein molecules

**developed countries**: countries in the industrialized world; highly economically and technologically developed

**developing countries**: countries that are economically and technologically less developed

**diabetics**: people suffering from disorders linked to insufficient insulin production

**embryo**: name for the early stages of a fertilized egg, as it divides and grows

**enzymes**: proteins capable of producing chemical changes in organic substances

**fermentation**: a chemical change brought about by enzymes, such as the conversion of grape sugar into ethyl alcohol by yeast

**fertilizers**: substances used to make soil rich and productive

**genes**: coded messages stored along the DNA of a chromosome

**hemophiliacs**: people suffering from a genetic disorder causing excessive bleeding from minor injuries, due to an absence of the clotting factor in blood

**immune system**: the complex network that protects the body against disease

**insecticides**: substances or preparations used for killing insects

**in vitro fertilization**: a technique by which an egg is fertilized with a sperm in a laboratory dish and then implanted in a uterus for gestation

**messenger RNA (mRNA)**: RNA formed from a DNA template that enters the cytoplasm, where its genetic code specifies the amino acid sequence for protein production

**nematode worm**: an unsegmented roundworm that is often parasitic on animals and plants

**offspring**: the children, or descendants, of a particular set of parents

**parthenogenesis**: the development of an egg without fertilization

**pesticides**: chemicals that destroy plant, fungal, or animal pests

**replicate**: to reproduce or duplicate

**sickle cell anemia**: a hereditary disease in which an accumulation of oxygen-deficient cells results in anemia, blood clotting, or joint pain

**vaccines**: preparations of weakened or killed bacteria or viruses introduced into the body to stimulate immunity to disease

# Index

# *Photo Credits*

**Cover**: Sperm, Colored Blue, at the Point of Fusion With a Human Egg (**Wellcome Trust Medical Photographic Library, Yorgos Nikas**); **Title Page**: Eyewire Inc.; **Lester V. Bergman/CORBIS/ MAGMA**: page 22; **Scott Camazine**: pages 14, 18; **Camera Press, Barrington Brown**: page 15; **Corel**: page 34; **DigitalVision**: pages 20, 26, 39; **Mike Grandmaison**: page 32; **Kindra Clineff Photography**: page 27; **Katherine Phillips** (illustration): page 4; **Popperfoto/Reuters**: page 17; **Reuters NewMedia Inc./CORBIS/MAGMA**: page 44; **Harry Soltes/Seattle Times**: page 41; **E. Melanie Watt**: page 8; **The Wellcome Trust, P. Artymiuk/Wellcome Photo Library**: page 10; **R. Errington, S. Davies & P.J. Smith/Wellcome Photo Library**: page 25; **Sanger Centre/Wellcome Photo Library**: page 13; **V. Subramanian/Wellcome Trust Photographic Library**: page 40; **T.J. McMaster/Bristol Physics SPM Unit/Wellcome Trust Photo Library**: page 47; **Wellcome Photo Library**: pages 2/3, 16, 21; **Wellcome Trust Medical Photographic Library**: page 6; **Yorgos Nikas/Wellcome Photo Library**: page 36; **Yorgos Nikas/Wellcome Trust Photo Library**: page 42.